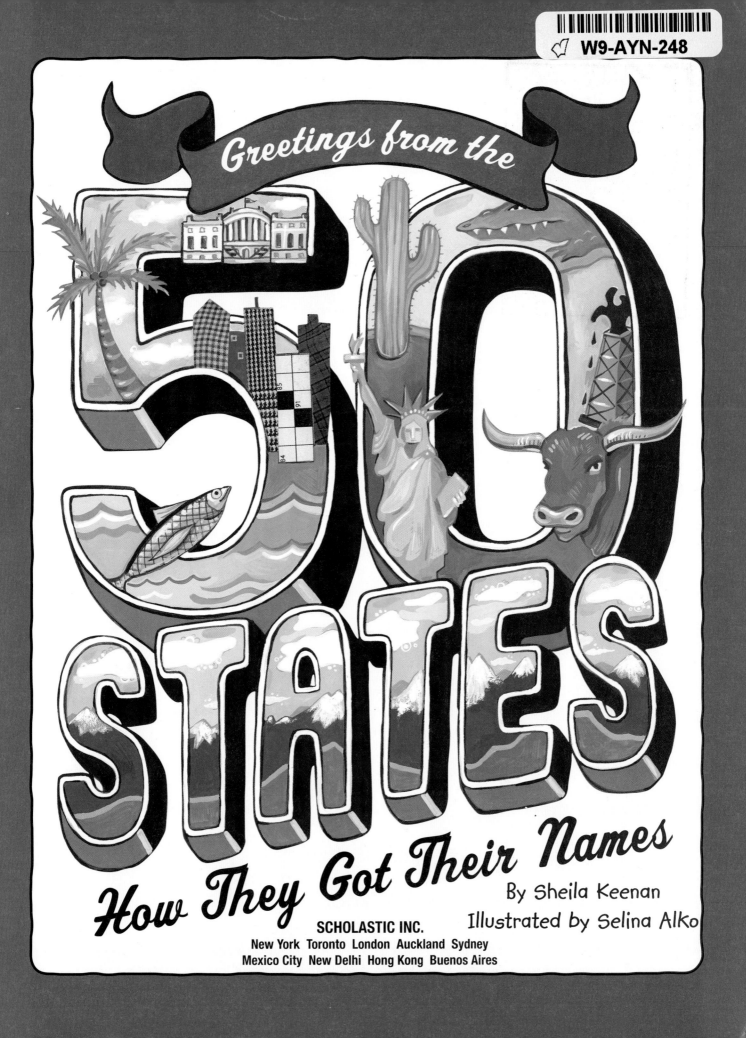

Greetings from the

50 STATES

How They Got Their Names

By Sheila Keenan

Illustrated by Selina Alko

SCHOLASTIC INC.
New York Toronto London Auckland Sydney
Mexico City New Delhi Hong Kong Buenos Aires

For Kevin: On the road again, I just can't wait to get on the road again . . .

Many thanks to Kate Waters for yet another wonderful editorial enterprise; to Brenda Murray for her unflagging enthusiasm and help with this book; to Erin Black for pitching in; to Becky Terhune and Kay Petronio for the beautiful design work; and to Selina Alko for the cool, cool geography visuals! —S.K.

To Sean, Isaiah, and Ginger, with love; and to Ben, Kay, and the group for guiding me on my journey of self-discovery here in the United States. —S.A.

ISBN-13: 978-0-545-16136-7
ISBN-10: 0-545-16136-3

10 9 8 7 6 5 4 3 2 1   9 10 11 12 13 14/0

Printed in the U.S.A.   40

This edition first printing, January 2009

Book design by Kay Petronio

Contents

The Name Game

It could have happened.

These are names once used for New Jersey, Hawaii, New York, and Nevada. Whose idea was that? Try a British King, an English sea captain, a Dutch trading company, and a miner who may have read *The Hunchback of Notre Dame*.

To find out how our 50 states and the District of Columbia were named, you have to time travel through American history, going back more than 500 years to when the full-scale European exploration of our country began. These explorers, settlers, missionaries, and entrepreneurs came looking for (choose one or more):

○ a passage to China and the Indies

○ *gold*

○ a good place for a colony

○ *gold*

○ souls to save

○ *gold*

○ fish, fur, and timber

○ Did we mention *gold*?

Of course, the United States wasn't one big blank map waiting for the Europeans to come fill in the missing names and borders. There were millions and millions of Native Americans living in North America when Columbus arrived in 1492. That's a lot of people who already had words for themselves, their cities, settlements, hunting grounds, mountains, plains, rivers, and streams. This explains why 27 state names come from Native American words . . . or at least what the Spanish, French, English, Portuguese, or Dutch *thought* they heard the Indians say. Tribal names were often spelled phonetically by Europeans using their own languages. Then as English-speaking people spread across the country, they often respelled place names in their language and *voilà!* — you end up with 24, maybe even 80 different spellings of Kansas, for example.

What *else* was in play in the name game besides tribal languages? Royalty, red, and romance.

Romance?

Yup! Our third largest state may be named after a mythical place in a Spanish romance novel. Two other states are named for the color red. And as for royalty? Say you wanted to get in good with your king or queen so they'll keep financing your expeditions or set you up with a colony. Wouldn't they just love it if you or your trusty representative sailed over to America, "discovered" and claimed a huge chunk of land (ignoring the tribes who were already there), and gave the place their royal name?

You bet they would; in fact, sometimes the monarchs spelled it out in writing: Name the place after me. Seven states can give themselves royal airs over their names. Oddly enough, that's six more than are named after a U.S. president.

Behind each state's name is a story of how Americans felt about the land they settled in, how they connected to its history and geography, how they recognized its unique character, how proud they felt of themselves and their state. That's true for a state's nickname, too.

Well, it's usually true.

Okay, sure, who wants to say they're from the Mosquito State or the Web-footed State or the Mud-waddler State or the Stub-toe

State? Luckily, those aren't the *official* nicknames for New Jersey, Oregon, Mississippi, and Montana; they all have perfectly respectable other nicknames. Many states have more than one nickname, some official, some unofficial but widely used.

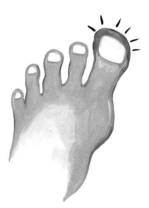

So what's in a state name or nickname?

Plenty!

Let's go on a cross-country trip to find out where all those big names on our map came from.

Things to Know Before You Go...
deeper into this book.

⭐ The 50 states are arranged alphabetically; Washington, D.C., follows at the end. Each entry includes information about the state's name, nickname, and the year it was granted statehood.

⭐ Historically, there were many different ways to spell the same place name. The most common spellings are used here.

⭐ Quoted material is from the primary source mentioned in an entry. That's the beauty of the Internet: you can go online and read the *Charter for the Province of Pennsylvania* and see exactly what "CHARLES the Second by the Grace of God King of England, Scotland, France and Ireland" had to say to "Our Trustie and wellbeloved Subject WILLIAM PENN" in 1681. Some good Web sites: The Avalon Project at Yale Law School, www.yale.edu/lawweb/avalon; Library of Congress, www.loc.gov; National Archives and Records, www.archives.gov.

⭐ The full history of a state and its original native inhabitants could never fit in a book this size. That would be like writing your life story on a postcard. So when you get to the last page, check the list of Web sites to find out where you can read more about the great states of our United States.

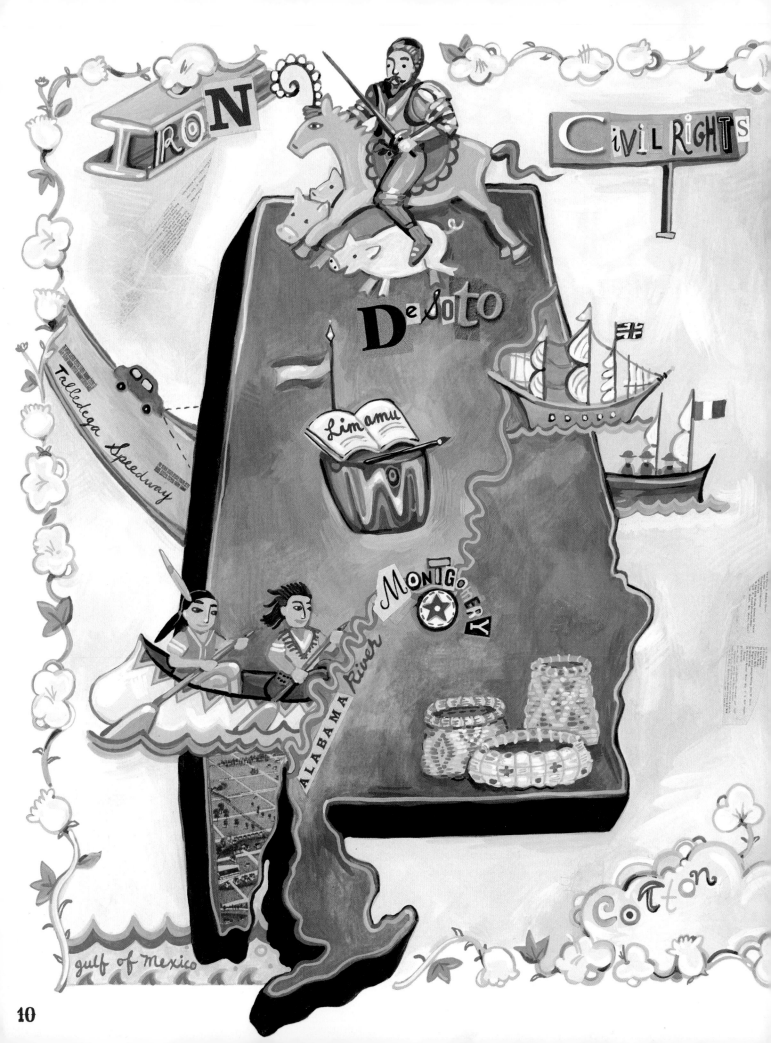

IRON

CiViL RiGHTS

Talledega Speedway

DeSoto

Limamu

Montgomery

ALABAMA River

gulf of Mexico

COTTON

Alabama

Sweet Home Alabama. Or is that Alebamon? Allibamou anyone?

There are 31 different spellings recorded for this southern state. It all depended on which Spanish, French, or British explorer or settler was taking the notes.

The name was first recorded by three gentlemen who traveled with the Spanish conquistador Hernando de Soto. In 1540, de Soto came tromping through Alabama with his horses, dogs, herd of pigs, and gold-hungry, plundering army. One gentleman's written account tracked the expedition through *Alibamu;* the other man penned *Alibamo.* De Soto's secretary was even more geographically creative: He wrote *Limamu* in his diary.

No matter how you spell it, Alabama isn't a European name anyhow. The resident Choctaw probably called their farming neighbors the Alabama from the Choctaw *alba* for "plants" or "vegetation" and *amo* for "gatherer." The Alabama River got its name from the tribe; the state got its name from the river. (And the movie got its name from the song!)

You'll find "Heart of Dixie" on everything from souvenir T-shirts to Alabama license plates. Dixie is a nickname for the South or for the Confederate states. The word may have come from old $10 bills called dixies, which were used before the Civil War.

1860

10 *Heart of Dixie State*

1860 **DIXIE DOLLARS** 10

MT. McKINLEY

midnight sun

Arctic OCEAN

RUSSIA

RANGE
MOUNTAIN

SEWARD
PENINSULA

"We were many, now we are few"

oil   GOLD

BERING
Sea

KING SALMON

ALASKA PENINSULA

JUNeau

500
miles to
U.S.
mainland

ALáXsXaq

PACIFIC   OCEAN

12

Alaska

Alaska has 34,000 miles of shoreline. No wonder it got its name from *aláxsxaq*, the Aleutian word for "shore" or "that toward which the sea is directed." The Aleut are one of the native peoples of Alaska. At first, their word and others like it — *agunalaksh, al-ak-shak,* or *al-ay-ek-sa* — were used only for the Alaskan peninsula that juts into the chilly Bering Sea. Russians and Americans who migrated and took over former tribal lands in the 18th and 19th centuries began to use the word *Alaska* for the whole 586,400 square miles of what became our 49th state.

Seward's Folly. Seward's Ice Box. Icebergia. The Polar Bear Garden. Alaska's early nicknames were a joke. That's because many people thought U.S. Secretary of State William H. Seward was a fool to pay Russia $7,200,000 in gold in 1867 for the vast, frozen, unexplored wilderness it owned in the far north. The territory was so remote, it wasn't even connected to the U.S. mainland.

Then in the 1880s, prospectors struck gold in Alaska. Nobody was laughing at Seward anymore, especially since he'd only paid 2.5 cents an acre for the whole gigantic state!

Alaska's modern nicknames, the Last Frontier or the Land of the Midnight Sun, honor the northern state's beautiful, rugged landscape, and long — *really long* — Arctic summer days.

2.5¢ *Last Frontier State*

13

Arizona

Once there was a small spring out west called *Alehzon* by the Pima who lived near it. The Spaniards came exploring in the 16th century and eventually called these Pima tribal lands *Arizonac*, a variation on native words.

At least, that's the most common explanation. Others say "the place of the small spring" might have been called *Ali-Shonak*. Or Arizona may have come from Spanish words for "arid place."

Wet or dry, the name *Arizona* took. And a silver miner helped make it official.

Charles D. Poston was a mining entrepreneur who loved the place: "The valleys of Arizona are not surpassed for fertility and beauty by any that I have seen, and that includes the whole world." In 1862, Poston went to Washington, D.C., chatted up President Lincoln, threw a lovely oyster dinner for some congressmen who wanted to move out west to help the "galoots" (and their own flagging careers), and got a bill passed officially recognizing the Arizona Territory.

In 1857–1858, Lieutenant Joseph Ives led an expedition for the U.S. War Department. He surveyed parts of the American West, including some of what is now Arizona. Lieutenant Ives reached the southern rim of the Grand Canyon. He predicted no other party would come to visit this "profitless locality," which he declared "altogether valueless . . ."

Altogether WRONG!

Today, nearly 5,000,000 people a year come to the Grand Canyon State to see one of the natural wonders of the world.

Grand Canyon State

Arkansas

Arkansas became our 25th state on June 15, 1836.

There oughta be a law about Arkansas — and there is!

In the 19th century, you'd probably say you were from ARkanSAW, but your fellow Americans would claim you hailed from ArKANSAS. Even Arkansas's two U.S. senators couldn't agree on where they came from.

Phonics and spelling saved the day! In 1881, the state legislature passed a bill that declared the state's name would be spelled Arkansas, but pronounced "Arkansaw."

The original confusion shows what happens when French-speaking explorers tangle with tribal names. In the 17th century, the French met up with native people who lived west of the Mississippi River. They called themselves the Ugakhpa or "those going downstream"; Quapaw was also used; and Algonquian-speakers called them Arkansas, meaning "south wind." The explorers wrote down the Indian names as they heard them — and of course, they were writing in French. At one time, there were around 70 variations, from Aksansea to Acansa.

It's had two pronunications, so why not two official nicknames? The Land of Opportunity was adopted in 1947 to encourage businesses and tourism. In 1995, the Arkansas legislature decided the Natural State was a better way to promote the state's "unsurpassed scenery" and "abundant wildlife."

OZARK mountains

Natural State

California

In the early 16th century, Spanish adventurers —
looking for treasure as usual — sailed to what they
thought was an island. The explorer Hernán Cortés called it California.

He probably got the name out of a book.

Las Sergas de Esplandián (*The Adventures of Esplandian*), written by García
Ordóñez de Montalvo, was a very popular Spanish novel of the time. It was filled
with romance, chivalry, and fantastic tales of California, the "strangest island of
the world." This legendary California was paradise: It was laden with gold and
strewn pearls; it was inhabited only by brave, beautiful women, who harnessed wild
beasts and galloped around waving golden weapons. (Ordóñez de Montalvo would
have loved Hollywood!)

Mapmakers started labeling the "island" on the Pacific coast *California*. The
name stuck even though later explorers and missionaries proved the "island" was
a pensinsula, now Baja California in Mexico, and that the rest of California was on
the mainland.

The Spaniards weren't the only ones looking to get rich quick in California.
Thousands of people rushed there after precious nuggets of gold
were discovered in 1848. The fevered California Gold Rush
tops the list of what makes this the Golden State.

Golden
State

19

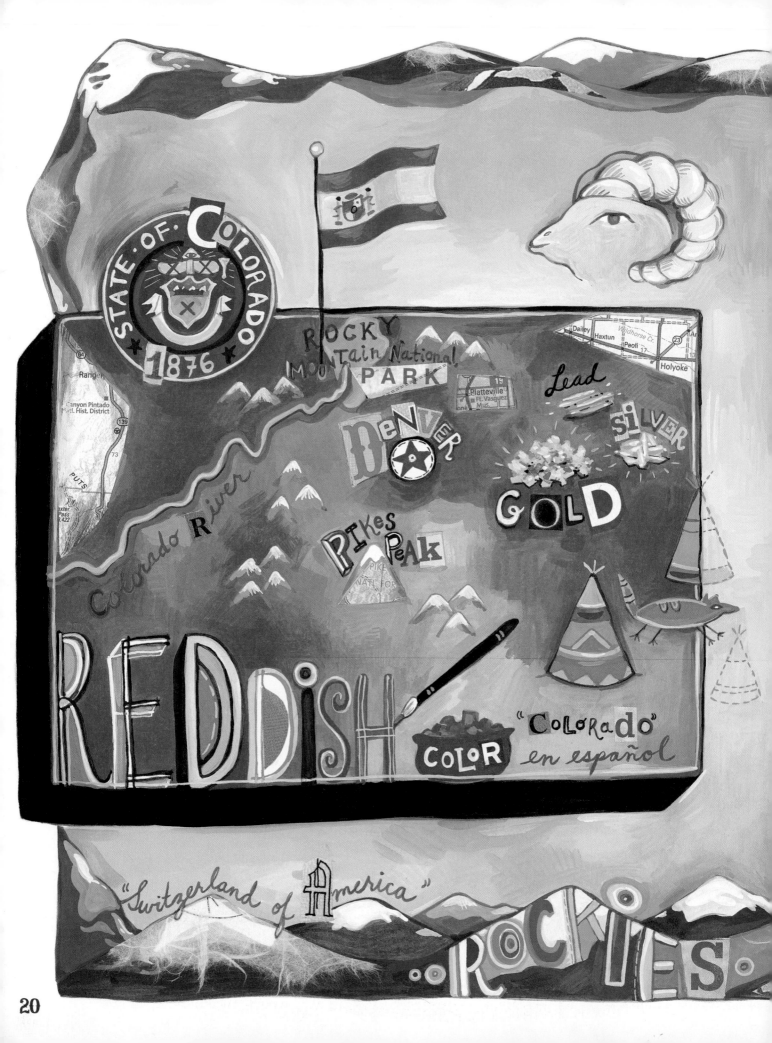

20

Colorado

Who's in favor of naming this place Idaho?

No, that's a coined word.

Jefferson?

Okay, but, it's a temporary thing only.

Colorado?

Si! That's a great name for a state.

The Spanish were the first Europeans to reach this western state; they got here in the 16th century. *Colorado* means "reddish color" in Spanish. It was a good, descriptive name for the area because of the warm, earthy color of its land and river.

Over the next 200 years, trappers and settlers eventually pushed out the native peoples. New geographic names such as Osage, Colona, and Idaho were considered and rejected. From 1859 to 1861, Colorado temporarily organized itself as the Territory of Jefferson. But gold, not red, became the name of the game.

Gold was discovered near what is now Denver; the mountains were full of silver and lead, too. The rush was on!

The boom territory soon wanted to be part of the Union. Congress was happy to officially recognize such a rich region as the Colorado Territory in 1861.

Colorado's nickname, the Centennial State, shows good timing. It became a state in 1876, the same year the United States celebrated the hundredth anniversary of the signing of the Declaration of Independence. It's also called the Switzerland of America. Colorado's Rocky Mountains have more than 1,000 peaks that top 10,000 feet.

Centennial State

Connecticut

If you were in a spelling bee and were asked to spell the word from which we got Connecticut, you could win with *Quinnehtukqut* . . . or *Quinnihticut* or even *Quonehtacut*.

No matter how it is written in English, this Mohegan word means "beside the long tidal river." The native people used the word as the river's name; in the 1600s, European explorers and colonists used it to mean the area that became the state.

The *Quonehtacut* or Connecticut River is indeed long: At 410 miles, it's the longest river in New England and flows through or passes by four states: New Hampshire, Vermont, Massachusetts, and Connecticut. Maritime history was made on its waters. In 1776, David Bushnell launched an amazing invention on the Connecticut: the *American Turtle*, a submarine!

Because of the river, Connecticut became a thriving manufacturing state. Industry made Connecticuters famous for their — what else? — industriousness. People called the state the Land of Steady Habits.

Nearly 150 years before our Constitution was written, settlers in Connecticut adopted The Fundamental Orders. This 1639 document declared Connecticut would govern itself by "the free consent of the people." This is sometimes called the first written constitution in history. And in Connecticut, they agree: It's officially the Constitution State.

Unofficially, it's the Nutmeg State. A nutmeg looks like a nut, but is actually a very, very hard fruit seed that's used as a spice. Colonial Connecticut "nutmeggers" peddled these seeds; some customers didn't realize you had to grate them and thought they had been sold wooden goods.

Nutmeg State

Delaware

Our tale opens with a terrible storm.

In 1610, the English explorer Samuel Argall was on a mission to bring supplies to the desperate, starving colonists in Jamestown, Virginia. Bad weather blew him off course into an unfamiliar bay. Captain Argall named the bay and the river that flowed into it Delaware, after Lord De La Warr, the English colonial governor of Virginia. The governor, who was waiting in Virginia, was no doubt honored. But he was probably even happier when Argall and his boatload of goods got back on course.

The Delaware River and Delaware Bay lap at the coastline of the state that eventually inherited the same name.

Delaware may be the second smallest state, but it's the proud First State. That's because on December 7, 1787, Delaware became the first state to ratify the U.S. Constitution.

Just because you're a small state that's not quite 2,000 square miles, doesn't mean you're not big enough for *several* nicknames. Delaware is also called the:

DIAMOND STATE

You won't get rich hunting diamonds here. This nickname comes from Thomas Jefferson. The founding father and president said that Delaware was a small, valuable jewel because of its important location on the East Coast.

BLUE HEN STATE

Sounds like a cute name from a heartwarming animal story, right? Probably not. It may refer to chickens used in game fights that were popular with Revolutionary War soldiers. The Blue Hen Chicken was a scrappy fighter and a winning breed, so some Delaware soldiers took to calling themselves after the bird. However, no one's really sure where the nickname comes from.

Blue Hen State

Florida

The 16th-century Spanish explorer Juan Ponce de León was looking for the mythical fountain of youth whose magical waters were said to make you stay forever young.

He found Florida — and death.

Ponce de León landed on the northeast coast of the state on April 2, 1513. As explorers are apt to do, he claimed the whole place and then gave it a name: Florida.

Pascua florida was the Spanish feast of the flowers held at Eastertime. April was Eastertime. The newfound land was lush with flowers, trees, shrubs, and blooming vines; *florida* also means flowery, so Ponce de León figured he had picked the perfect name.

Alas! Plants were his undoing.

In 1521, Ponce de León and his men were scouting good locations for a Spanish colony in Florida. They were attacked by a band of Calusa who already lived there. The Calusa dipped their arrows in sap from the manchineel tree. This tree is so poisonous that if a raindrop slides down a manchineel leaf and then drips onto your skin, you'll get burning blisters. When Ponce de León was pierced by a Calusa's poison arrow, he didn't stand a chance.

Pick up a travel brochure for Florida and you'll see white sandy beaches, sunny blue skies, palm trees. Tourism is one of Florida's main businesses, hence the official nickname: the Sunshine State.

Then there's the fun nickname, the Alligator State. Spanish explorers called them *largatos* (lizards). Gators live in just about any body of freshwater in Florida: rivers, lakes, swamps, marshes, and the state's unique Everglades. There were once so many alligators in Florida, an 18th-century writer said you could cross a river on their heads, "had the animal been harmless."

Alligator State

STATE OF GEORGIA
CONSTITUTION
JUSTICE
1776

13th British Colony

THE GOOBER STATE

ATLANTA

n-guba

tailor

Carpenter

Columbus

King George II

Savannah

Baker

X Debt

Okefenokee Refuge

James Oglethor

ATLANTIC

Georgia

This state is named after a rich English King who wished to "relieve the wants of our . . . poor subjects."

Of course, there was something in it for His Highness, too.

In 1732, King George II of England granted a charter to James Oglethorpe, a British philanthropist, for what became the 13th British colony in America. The King spelled out the name of the new colony in this charter: Georgia, in honor of . . . himself. King George II hoped that Georgia, once settled, would "increase the trade, navigation and wealth of our realms." It would also help prevent its British colonial neighbor, South Carolina, from being overrun by Spanish colonists from Florida.

Originally, Oglethorpe planned Georgia as a place where poor people could resettle instead of suffering and dying in British prisons because of their debts. It was a noble idea, but there were plenty of people outside jail willing to head for America. Oglethorpe set sail on November 17, 1732, with 115 men, women, and children. They included carpenters, tailors, a baker, a basketmaker, a heelmaker, and one William Little, who "understands flax and hemp."

There were no debtors.

Peaches or peanuts? Take your pick. Georgia is called the Peach State or the Goober State because these are the state's big cash crops.

Goober is another word for peanut. It comes from the African *n-guba*, a word used in several Bantu tribal languages. The word and the nuts came to North America with enslaved Africans. Georgia produces more than two billion pounds of peanuts a year — not to mention the world's largest peach cobbler, a tasty dessert that uses 250 pounds of sugar, 300 pounds of flour, and 75 gallons of peaches.

Peach State

Hawaii

Hawaii became our 50th state on August 21, 1959.

Even if you're a remote chain of volcanic islands in the Pacific Ocean thousands of miles from any mainland, sooner or later some curious explorer sails by and, naturally, gives you a name.

Tradition and history say this happened to Hawaii . . . twice!

According to ancient stories, Hawai'i Loa, an island chief and fearless fisherman, paddled his canoe around the Pacific, following the stars. He eventually reached a chain of islands, landed on the shores of the easternmost one, and named it after himself: Hawai'i. The chief later brought over his family and settled the beautiful island. En route, he named the other islands in the chain after his children.

In 1778, another boatman also reached Hawaii, but he came in a sloop. Captain James Cook, an English explorer, visited the Hawaiian islands and promptly named them the Sandwich Islands, in honor of his patron, the Earl of Sandwich.

Not everyone liked the name.

By 1810, King Kamehameha I united the formerly independent islands. He referred to his kingdom as the Islands of the King of Hawai'i. The kingdom became a republic, which became a U.S. territory, then finally a state. The name — with and without the apostrophe — survived.

If you've ever received a postcard from Hawaii, you know why many people call it the Paradise of the Pacific. But Hawaii is officially called the Aloha State. *Aloha* isn't Hawaiian slang for "hi." It's a word with several spiritual and emotional meanings. According to the 1959 state law that established Hawaii's popular name, "Aloha Spirit" is "the coordination of mind and heart within each person."

Aloha State

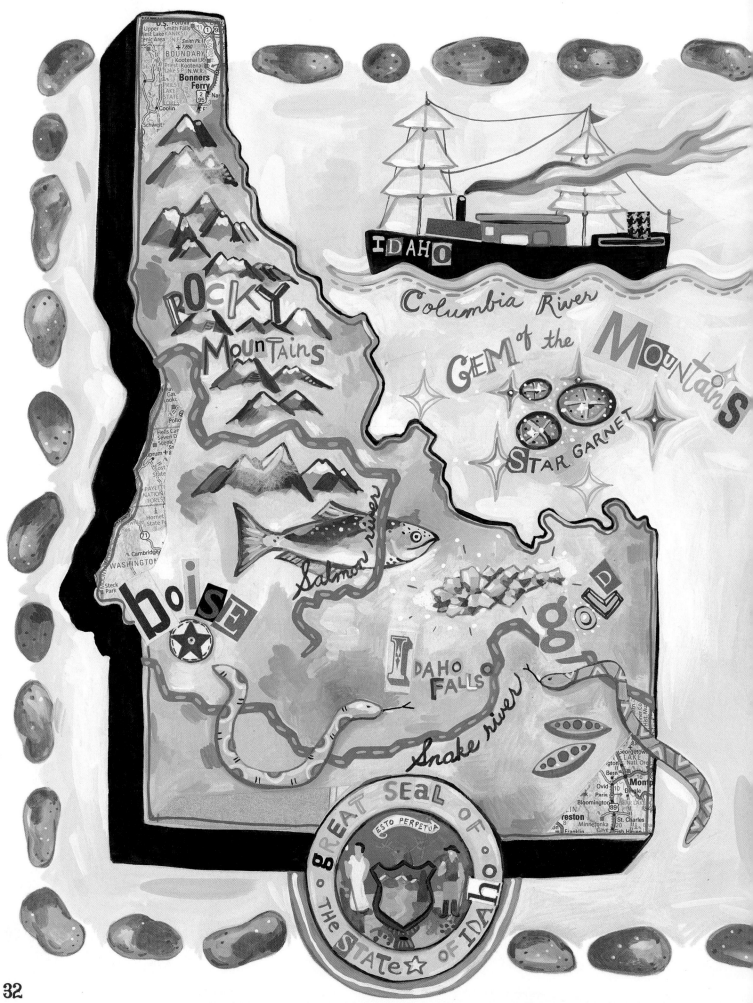

Idaho

Idaho became our 43rd state on July 3, 1890.

George M. Willing, a 19th-century mining lobbyist, had a way with words. He claimed Idaho was an Indian term that meant "gem of the mountains."

He didn't say which Indians.

Idaho was the perfect name for a booming Rocky Mountain territory, Willing suggested, especially one that included the rich mining area Pikes Peak. People in the area, even Congress, were willing to go along . . . until they found out Idaho wasn't really a Native American word. It wasn't even really a word; Willing had invented it himself. The U.S. Senate called the territory Colorado instead.

Meanwhile, "Idaho" traveled to the Northwest. In the 1860s, a steamboat named *The Idaho* chugged up and down the Columbia River. Towns like Idaho Springs sprang up. Gold was discovered in the area, and people rushed to what were soon called the Idaho mines. In a few short years, no one cared about where the word came from, it suited where they were just fine. In 1863, Congress went with Idaho when it designated the territory that became our 43rd state.

Gem of the Mountains stuck. It's true Idaho is known for its rare purple gem, the star garnet. But it's even more famous for another underground prize: spuds. Idaho, the Potato State, grows more of this crop than any other state. We're talking 13.8 billion pounds of spuds a year!

Potato State

Father Jacques Marquette — windy city — Chicago

LAKE MICHIGAN

Van Buren — to North Michigan Ave — Chicago

PeORiA — Illinois River

ILLinOiS people

Corn

SPRingFiELD

Jacksonville

the LanD of Lincoln

the Prairie STAte

34

Illinois

In the 17th century, French explorers reached part of the homeland of the Illinois, a confederacy that included about 12 or 13 independent tribes. The Illinois shared many things in common, including the Algonquian language. As was often the case, not everything translated clearly between native peoples and newcomers. The Illinois, for example, called themselves "inoca."

Father Jacques Marquette, one of the first European explorers to reach Illinois, wrote in 1674 that the name of the people, which he transcribed as *Ilinois*, meant "the men," and was intended to elevate the Illinois above other native peoples. Illinois has also been translated as "warrior" or "tribe of superior men." The French commonly used it for the Native Americans they met within this area. So it made sense to French explorer René-Robert Cavelier, Sieur de La Salle, to use it on his river journey in 1679. La Salle called the waterway he sailed on the Illinois River. He built Fort Crèvecoeur, which means "Heartbreak," on the river, near present-day Peoria, Illinois. From there, La Salle and his crew of Frenchmen and Native Americans hopped in canoes and paddled downstream on into the Mississippi River.

But that's another story — Louisiana's story, actually!

Tall grass and a tall president gave this state two nicknames. Informally, Illinois is called the Prairie State, after the wide swaths of flatland filled with tall, coarse grasses and other prairie plants.

Officially, Illinois is known as the Land of Lincoln in honor of the state's favorite adopted son, President Abraham Lincoln. Lincoln moved to Illinois as a young man. There he worked his way up from clerk to congressman.

The rest is history.

IN GOD WE TRUST
Land of Lincoln
LIBERTY
1999 D

Indiana

Indiana became our 19th state on December 11, 1816.

In 1800, Congress passed a resolution that created a new U.S. territory. The act, approved and signed by President John Adams, created a new territory out of what is now Indiana, Illinois, Michigan, Wisconsin, and part of Minnesota. Congress declared this region "shall be called the Indiana Territory."

Indiana. Land of the Indians.

Indiana Territory was indeed home to many tribal groups: the Miami, the Potawatomi, the Kickapoo, the Mascouten, the Delaware (Lenni-Lenape), and the Shawnee.

The Indiana territorial government wanted people to come settle the area. They encouraged people to buy farmland on credit. Meanwhile, most Native Americans moved or were removed from Indiana Territory. The name remained.

Indianans are proud to be from the Hoosier State. But where "hoosier" comes from, nobody knows for sure. Hoosier could be a contraction of "Who's yere?," a common reply if you knocked on a cabin door during Indiana's pioneer days. Or it could come from "husher," slang for tough brawling Indiana riverboat men who hushed up their foes by beating them in fights.

Hoosier State

GRANT WOOD

IOWA fur pelts

Sioux City

FARMLAND

Iowa River

DesMoiNes

pie

eggs

MiDDLE of AmericA

milk

bread

Iowa

Iowa became our 29th state on December 28, 1846.

It's all about geography and history, with a little bit of spelling thrown in.

The state of Iowa is named after the Iowa River. The river was named after the native peoples living near its banks. Here's where spelling comes in.

French explorers called the tribal people they met in the river area the Ayuwha. By the 1700s, the Ayuwha and French traders were doing business. Bartering brought European goods like glass beads, iron knives, and gun parts to the Indian villages; the French took away valuable fur pelts. By the 1800s, British entrepreneurs and American colonists had moved in. They called the tribe they traded with the Ioway or Iowa.

White settlement of Iowa began in earnest in 1833. The Ioway, like other Native American groups in the United States, were soon pushed off their lands. Iowa became home to more pioneer Iowans than Native American Ioways.

The most common nickname for Iowa is the Hawkeye State.

But why Hawkeye?

One claim is that it's in honor of Chief Black Hawk, a courageous Sauk war chief. Black Hawk and his people had been forced to give up their land in Illinois and move to Iowa. In 1832, the chief fought back . . . he lost. Six years later, editor James G. Edwards named his newspaper the *Burlington Hawk-eye*. Edwards and his friend, Judge David Rorer, promoted the name in honor of the man who had tried to save his land and people.

Others say the name honors Natty "Hawkeye" Bumppo, the fearless scout in James Fenimore Cooper's popular American novel *The Last of the Mohicans* (1826).

CHIEF BLACK HAWK

Hawkeye State

Kansas

KaNze, the word source of this state's name, looks like it could be a hip-hop label. Actually, it's a Native American tribal word, which may mean "south wind."

It's easy to see how *KaNze* became Kansa or Kansas when the French explorers who crossed the great plains of this state and floated down its waterways started taking notes and drawing maps.

As more European explorers and then American settlers headed west and spelled things *their* way, the confusion about the name increased. Some sources say there could be as many as 125 different spellings of this tribe's name, from Can to Keniser to Escanzaques.

The Kansas, who are also commonly called the Kaw, were buffalo hunters who maintained villages near what came to be called the Kansas River. Eventually the region also became known as Kansas. The Kansas-Nebraska Act of 1854 helped standardize the spelling. It also led to Kansas's historical nickname. The congressional act said that the people of the territories Kansas and Nebraska could decide for themselves whether or not to allow slavery within their borders. Since the territories wanted to apply for statehood, what the Kansans and Nebraskans decided would affect the entire Union. Pro-slavery and antislavery forces rushed into Kansas. These settlers wanted to sway the vote — and they didn't just stick to the ballot box. Violent clashes broke out across "Bleeding Kansas."

Modern Kansas has a cheerier nickname, the Sunflower State. Bright yellow wild sunflowers grow like weeds across Kansas. The 1903 law that made *Helianthus annuus* the official state flower praised the sunflower as "richly emblematic of the majesty of a golden future."

Sunflower State

Kentucky

Kentucky came from words in any one of several Native American languages. Interpretations of these tribal word sources vary from "prairie" to "great meadow" to "land of tomorrow." Land of opportunity is how many people looked at this central state bounded by rivers and mountains on three sides.

Kentucky was traditionally a rich hunting ground for several major Native American groups, including the Shawnee, the Chickasaw, and the Cherokee. It was a political bargaining chip for the Spanish, French, and English who each made claims on it in the 17th and 18th centuries. Colonel Richard Henderson tried to buy a big chunk of it from the Cherokee in an enterprising, but illegal, real-estate trade in 1775. He offered 10,000 English pounds worth of guns, blankets, clothes, rum, and other trading goods. A group of Cherokee leaders agreed to sell him 20 *million* acres of land. Virigina, which claimed Kentucky itself, nixed the deal. And let's not forget Daniel Boone and all the pioneers who followed him down the Wilderness Road and settled Kentucky.

The grass is greener in the Bluegrass State. Kentucky bluegrass really has green blades, but its buds are blue-purple, hence the name. Bluegrass seeds came along with the pioneers and their grazing animals. As the people spread out, so did the grass, growing what Native Americans called white man's tracks. Bluegrass is also a form of stringed American country music, popularized by Kentucky's own mandolin-playing Bill Monroe, the late great "Father of Bluegrass Music."

Bluegrass State

44

Louisiana

Gumbo is a spicy Louisiana stew that mixes a French base with a dash of Spanish, a dollop of African, and a pinch of American flavors.

This state is just like its famous stew.

Louisiana was home to many Native American peoples, including tribes of the Choctaw, Caddo, and Natchez nations. Then the Europeans came along and claimed huge parts of the Mississippi Valley.

Hernando de Soto explored the region and staked a claim for Spain in 1541; the Spanish pretty much left it at that. The intrepid French explorer, René-Robert Cavalier, Sieur de La Salle, started at the Great Lakes and traveled on down the entire Mississippi River. Along the way, he claimed the whole area for France in 1682. La Salle dubbed the river valley Louisiana, after the flamboyant French king Louis XIV.

For the next 121 years, European nations passed the Louisiana territory around like a big bowl of gumbo. France gave part of it to Spain; Great Britain snagged another section; Spain returned the colony to France; the French ruler Napoleon Bonaparte finally sold the Louisiana Territory to the United States in 1803 for $15,000,000. Nine years later, a portion of it became the state of Louisiana.

Louisiana is called the Pelican State because there once were so many of these cool birds flapping about. The brown pelican, which is the largest web-footed bird in the world, nearly died out in Louisiana because of pollution, but state conservation efforts have helped bring back pelican colonies.

Pelican State

Maine

Maine became our 23rd state on March 15, 1820.

Maine is the only state with a single-syllable name, and it's a pretty simple name at that. Finding out what it means is a lot more complicated.

There's the "land, ho!" explanation. Maine may come from "the main," Meyne, or Mayne, words that signified the mainland, as opposed to the more than 3,000 islands off the state's coast. French explorers, fishermen, and sailors like this explanation.

There's also the "I'm the king and I said so" explanation. In 1622, an English charter granted land it called "the province of Maine" to Sir Ferdinando Gorges and Captain John Mason. Mason spun off New Hampshire from this grant. In a 1639 charter, King Charles I made it clear to Sir Gorges what he was to do with his share: ". . . the Mayne Lande and Premises aforesaide shall forever hereafter bee called The Province or Countie of Mayne and not by any other name or names whatsoever."

Sir Gorges didn't get to pick a name for his landholding, but he was entitled to everything Maine had to offer, from lumber and fish to the "Wrecks of Shipps or Merchandize" that might wash up on its shores. Not a bad deal when you're talking around 3,500 miles of coastline.

Maine, the Pine Tree State, has 17 million acres of forest. How else would they be the leading producer of wooden toothpicks?

The official state tree, the white pine, is the largest conifer in the Northeast. No wonder colonial shipbuilders hewed them down and hauled them up as masts.

Pine Tree State

47

48

Maryland

Remember studying compound words? Remember underlining the small words inside the big word to make the meaning clear? Try it now.

Mary land. Got it. But who's Mary?

Maryland was named for Queen Henrietta Maria — Queen Mary for short — the wife of the English King Charles I. King Charles I granted the Maryland charter to Cecilius Calvert, the second Lord Baltimore, on June 20, 1632.

Lord Baltimore's father, George Calvert, had started the process of getting a colony from the King. The first Lord Baltimore thought Crescentia was a lovely name. Perhaps it was inspired by the crescent-shaped Chesapeake Bay that divides Maryland in two. But wisely the lord left the decision up to his lord; the King proposed *Terra Mariae*, Maryland. The King promised not to impose taxes on the residents of the Baltimores' colony, but in the charter, he did ask for a fifth of any gold or silver that might be unearthed and "Two Indian Arrows of these Parts, to be delivered at the said Castle of Windsor, every Year, on Tuesday in Easter Week."

You'll see Chesapeake State on some Maryland license plates, but it also has two historical nicknames, the Old Line State and the Free State.

General George Washington is said to have called Maryland the Old Line State in recognition of the bravery of Maryland's troops, the Maryland Line, during the Revolutionary War.

In 1923, a congressman from Georgia railed against Maryland as a traitor to the Union for not passing state laws to enforce the national Prohibition amendment banning alcohol. Hamilton Owens, a Maryland newspaper editor, ironically suggested that Maryland then just be its own Free State.

Old Line State

49

ATLANTIC

1620

Puritans

mayflower

Mus. of Antique Autos

Lancaster

Princeton   Sterling   Clinton

SALEm

blue Hills

MASSACHUSETTS

MASSACHUSETT BAY

BOSTON

Sharon   Mansfield   Easton

North Attleboro   Norton

PLYMOUTH   CAPE   COD   BAY

Cape Cod

MARTHA'S VINEYARD

MASSACHUSETTENSIS · SIGILLUM REIPUBLICAE

Massachusetts

Before the Puritans and the Pilgrims; before the French and Spanish cod fishers; before Leif Eriksson and his Norsemen; *long before the Red Sox,* there were "the people of the great hills," the Massachuset.

There are several ways to interpret the tribal name Massachuset, but they all pretty much include the same ideas: "near," "by," "great," "mountain," or "hill." Makes sense. This Native American group lived in and around the Blue Hills, a chain of 22 rises, including the 635-foot high Great Blue Hill near Boston. Their territory also extended south to Plymouth and north to Salem.

The Massachuset were few in number, made fewer by diseases brought over by European explorers and traders who sailed the Atlantic coast. Smallpox had wiped out 90% of the tribe's roughly 3,000 members by the time the Pilgrims arrived in 1620. When the Puritans established the Massachusetts Bay Colony several years later, only 500 or so Massachuset were still alive. As a separate tribe, the Massachuset did not survive their own name, which was given to the bay, the colony, and ultimately this New England state.

Massachusetts is nicknamed the Bay State (do the geography). It's also called the Baked Bean State. Puritans were strict about no cooking — pretty much no *anything* — on the Sabbath. So Puritan women whipped up hot *baked beans* on Saturday, which meant warm *baked beans* on Sunday morning . . . after church, of course.

Baked Bean State

Michigan

Michigan became our 26th state on January 26, 1837.

Michigan is surrounded by great lakes, four of them to be exact. Its name is connected to its unusual geography.

French explorers and traders first visited Michigan in the early 1600s. Their journals, letters, and early maps sometimes referred to place names already in use by the Native Americans who lived in the region. Many historians and linguists say Michigan comes from *michi-gama*, an Algonquian word that means "large lake" or "large body of water." A good name for a state washed by the waters of four of the five Great Lakes: Lake Michigan, Lake Superior, Lake Huron, and Lake Erie.

Other sources stay on dry land. They say Michigan comes from *majigan*, a Chippewa word for a clearing on the western side of the Lower Peninsula.

A wolverine is a fierce relative of the weasel, but a lot bigger and badder. They have large paws, sharp claws, and can chew through a cabin wall a foot thick.

So why would you nickname your state the Wolverine State?

A. There were a lot of wolverines wandering around Michigan. (Scientists and historians are still arguing about this.)

B. During the 1830s, Native Americans may have compared the settlers gobbling up their land to wolverines gobbling their food.

C. Michigan and Ohio were fighting over some land. Ohioans claimed the Michiganers were like bloodthirsty wolverines.

D. Any, all, or none of the above.

No one is sure where this unofficial nickname came from. So could we just use the other nickname instead? The Great Lake State sounds so much nicer.

Wolverine State

Minnesota

This midwestern state was traditionally home to the Dakota. They called one of the major rivers that flowed through their tribal lands *minisota*, "water that reflects the sky."

In the mid-1800s, thousands of European and American pioneers moved in and staked out their claims to timber-rich forests and tillable farmlands. The U.S. government forced the Dakota and other tribal people to give up their lands to make room for the new settlers.

By the late 1840s, the non-native people were clamoring for their own territory. A group of concerned citizens met in a store in Stillwater in 1848 to figure out how to get this territory recognized. Of course they also had to figure out what to call it. They considered presidential names like Washington or Jackson and tribal names like Chippewa or Algonquian. Itasca was suggested. The headwaters of the Mississippi River flow from Minnnesota's Lake Itasca. The name was coined by an American geologist from *veritas caput*, Latin for "truth" and "head."

The Stillwater delegates settled on a name already commonly used, added an "n" to change the pronunciation, and petitioned Congress to recognize the Minnesota Territory. Within a decade, Minnesota — still with two n's — became a state.

Minnesota is the Land of 10,000 Lakes — give or take a few lakes. The state actually has 11,842 lakes (the ones smaller than 10 acres don't count) and 6,564 streams and rivers, including the mighty Mississippi. All this water creates 90,000 miles of shoreline. No wonder one out of six Minnesotans owns a boat.

Land of 10,000 Lakes State

Mississippi

Quick! How many s's and p's are there in Mississippi?

This southern state, which is named after the famous Mississippi River that runs through it, is always a tough one to spell. Maybe it would have been easier if some of the original Native American names had been used instead.

Messipi, a name from the Algonquian language, means "great water." The Chippewa called the Mississippi *mici zibi*, meaning "great river" or "gathering in of all waters." That's certainly true: The Mississippi is joined by the Illinois, Missouri, Ohio, Arkansas, and Atchafalaya Rivers.

The Spanish and French who sailed and paddled along the Mississippi River in the 16th and 17th centuries, used a variety of names for the waterway, some based on Native American words. The French explorer, René-Robert Cavelier, Sieur de La Salle, may have been the first to put the name Mississippi on a map . . . literally. He labeled the river as such on a map made in 1695.

More than one hundred years later, Congress organized the Mississippi Territory, naming it after the river whose source is in Minnesota and mouth is in Louisiana.

Mississippi is called the Magnolia State after the state's official — and fragrant — state tree and state flower. Mississippi schoolchildren made this choice when they voted for the magnolia flower in 1900 and the magnolia tree in 1935.

Magnolia State

Missouri

Show me how to use Missouri three times in a sentence:

Missouri is named after the Missouri River, which is named after the Missouri.

The Missouri people were a small tribe whose name meant "people with the dugout canoes." They were among the Native Americans who were living in our 24th state when the Europeans arrived.

In 1673, the French explorer Louis Jolliet and the French missionary Father Jacques Marquette paddled their birch-bark canoe along the Mississippi River. They passed the mouth of a river: "So great was the agitation, that the water was very muddy, and could not become clear," Marquette later wrote in his journal.

That's why Native Americans called the river *pekitanoui*, which means "muddy water." Marquette, however, called this waterway the Missouri River on a map he made in 1673. This really muddied the waters and for a long time people misinterpreted the word *Missouri*. They mixed up the meaning of *pekitanoui* with the meaning of *Missouri*.

Ever drive behind a car with a Missouri license plate and wonder what they want you to show them? There are several different explanations for the state's unofficial nickname, the Show Me State. The most widely known one says it shows Missourians can't be fooled easily. Or as Missouri congressman Willard Duncan Vandiver put it at a dinner speech in 1899, ". . . frothy eloquence neither convinces nor satisfies me. I am from Missouri. You have got to show me."

Show Me State

Montana

Montana has more than 50 mountain ranges, including the magnificent Rocky Mountains. The word *montaanus* means "mountainous" in Latin; one Latinate form of this word is *montana*.

Montaanus. Montana. Get it?

Apparently Congress didn't.

A congressional committee met in February 1863 to discuss creating and naming a new western territory. James M. Ashley, a Republican representative from Ohio, suggested Montana. A senator didn't believe Montana was a real word; a Latin dictionary was produced as proof. Some congressmen wanted to use a Native American word, but couldn't think of the right one. Others played politics with the name: Democrats suggested Jefferson, after the third president and founder of their party; Republicans voted nay to that idea.

The name game ranged from Shoshone to Abyssinia until finally Congress reached an agreement. They settled on Ashley's original suggestion, Montana.

Montana's two main nicknames come from the earth below and the sky above. "Big Sky Country," found on the state's standard license plates, celebrates its wide-open spaces and wide-angle views. The phrase was inspired by A. B. "Bud" Guthrie, Jr.'s *The Big Sky*, a 1947 historical novel about the fur trade and the movement west.

Montana is also known as the Treasure State because of the rich gold, silver, and copper deposits that lured miners and mineral companies eager to strike it rich.

Treasure State

otoe

U of Nebraska

Omaha
"Ni-ubthatka"
"SPREADING WATER"

Nebrathka
"FLAT WATER"

Lieutenant Frémont

PLATTE River

LINCOLN Omaha

DUNDY 61
Rock Creek Lake St. Rec. Area
Parks 24 34

RICHARDS
Salem 8
Falls City

F · O · L · A · T

tree PLANters STATE

Nebraska

Nebraska is flat . . . in more ways than one.

The name of this Great Plains state comes down to us from its largest river and several languages. The Otoe called this 310-mile river *nebrathka*, meaning "flat water." French explorers and fur traders of the early 18th century used the Omaha name for the river, *ni-ubthatka*, which means "spreading water." They also gave it a French name, Platte River. Flat again.

Along comes Lieutenant John C. Frémont. He's on a mission for the U.S. government. The United States needs to get some pioneers settled out west before other countries, like England, take over the place. In 1842, Frémont explored the plains and Rocky Mountains with an eye toward opening it up for expansion. He wrote about the Platte River, using its Indian name. Frémont's report was the first time Nebraska appeared in print. Two years later, when the government was organizing this part of the country into a U.S. territory, the Secretary of War recommended it be called Nebraska because of the big, broad, and flat river that flowed through it.

Arbor Day started here in 1872, which made tree-planting an annual national activity and led to one of Nebraska's nicknames, the Tree Planters State.

Officially, Nebraska is the Cornhuskers State, after its state university football team and the old-school way of harvesting corn.

Corn-huskers State

Nevada

"¡Mira la sierra nevada!"

Spanish sailors checking out the scenery may have helped name our 36th state. As they sailed the Pacific from the Philippines to Mexico in the 1600s and 1700s, they spied whitecapped mountains along the way. *Sierra* means "saw-toothed mountain range," and *nevada* means "snow-covered" in Spanish. In 1776, Father Pedro Font, a member of a Spanish expedition, became the first to use the name on a map. The Sierra Nevada are technically in California; then again, before it became its own territory in 1861, Nevada had once belonged to California, as well as to Mexico and to Utah.

At a Nevada territorial convention in 1863, the delegates argued over what name to use when applying for statehood. The odds were against Nevada at first. The State of Washoe was a good bet. This name, which came from a local tribe, was popular with voters. Humboldt was proposed. So was a county name, Esmeralda. *Esmeralda* means "emerald" in Spanish; it's also the name of a female character in a popular French novel, *The Hunchback of Notre Dame*. In the end, the delegates chose Nevada.

Nevada was admitted to the Union toward the end of the Civil War, earning it the nickname the Battle Born State. It's also been called the Silver State. Nevada's famous Comstock Lode deposit yielded $400 million in silver and gold ore between 1859 and 1878. Comstock miners focused on digging for the gold at first and ignored the gray gunk that stuck to their shovels . . . until folks figured out that that gray was silver!

Silver State

SEAL of the STATE of NEW HAMPSHIRE * 1776 *

CANADA

PELTS

VERMONT

WHITE MOUNTAINS

Timber

Concord

Keene

CONCORD

MAINE

Captain John MASON

ENGLAND

HAMPSHIRE

ATLANTIC

MASSACHUSETTS

66

New Hampshire

Captain John Mason was a man with a plan. In 1629, the Londoner received a land grant for "makeing a plantation" on 60 miles of land in an area first called North Virginia by the explorer John Smith (Pocahontas's pal), then renamed New England by King James I (who clearly outranked Smith). Mason called his property New Hampshire, after Hampshire county in his native England.

Mason advertised for settlers and sent people over to start a fishing colony. New Hampshire isn't called the Mother of Rivers for nothing. The sources of five great New England rivers flow from its mountains. There were plenty of fish, not to mention fur pelts and timber.

Captain Mason spent a fortune on his investment in the wilderness. He had lands cleared, buildings erected, and intended to visit his "plantation." But his plans went awry: Mason died before he ever sailed for New Hampshire.

The little colony was later embroiled in some big boundary disputes. Massachusetts claimed part of New Hampshire; New Hampshire claimed most of Vermont; there was a land spat with New York and a border brouhaha with Quebec. Luckily for mapmakers, by 1842 New Hampshire's borders had finally been settled . . . except for a modern-day quarrel with Maine, which the U.S. Supreme Court ruled on in 2001.

New Hampshire is called the Granite State because there is so much of that igneous rock there. New Hampshire granite was used to build everything from curbs to the Library of Congress — where there's more than 30,000 tons of it!

Granite State

New Jersey

New Jersey was a hand-me-down. First it was home to the Lenni-Lenape. Then Dutch and Swedish settlers moved in, followed by the English, who took over.

In 1664, King Charles II of England passed along all the land between the Hudson and the Delaware Rivers to his brother James, the duke of York. The duke granted it to his two good friends, Lord John Berkeley and Sir George Carteret. The duke's charter called the place "New Caeserea or New Jersey." But Carteret came from the Isle of Jersey, a little island off the coast of England. He named his new lands in honor of his old home, where he had once been governor.

Berkeley and Carteret divided their land grant in half. Berkeley's "half" was almost twice as big as Sir George's share. No surprise: Some surveyors of the boundaries worked at night, when it's hard to see clearly and accurately; they used flaming tar barrels as markers. The noblemen owed the Duke of York 40 beaver skins and 20 gold coins rent a year for their New Jersey grant.

New Jersey officially became the Garden State in 1954, when the state legislature passed a bill adding it to car license plates. There are several interpretations of the nickname, but all of them have to do with New Jersey farms supplying food. (Beats the Clam State, a nickname tied to the Jersey Shore.)

Garden State

New Mexico

New Mexico became our 47th state on January 6, 1912.

You can trace this state's name all the way back to the Aztecs.

New Mexico is named after "old" Mexico. Mexico, the country south of the United States, got its name from Tenochtitlán, the capital city the Aztecs built in 1325. The Aztecs referred to themselves as Mexicas after the war god Mexitli. Their city was an amazing place built on an island. By the time Hernán Cortés first arrived there in 1519, Tenochtitlán was larger than any city in Europe at the time, with between 100,000 and 300,000 inhabitants. The Aztecs renamed their powerful capital Mexitli, in honor of the Aztec god of war. Mexico comes from Mexitli.

Spanish missionaries on an expedition in 1582 looking for Native Americans to convert are thought to be the first to have used *la Nueva Mejico* for what became our 47th state. Having a name inspired by a war god is fitting. Native Americans, Spanish conquistadors and settlers, the Mexican army, the U.S. army, Texans, cattlemen, and sheepherders all clashed over land, boundaries, and governance at one time or another in New Mexican history.

New Mexico officially became the Land of Enchantment on April 8, 1999. But the nickname has been around since 1935, when the tourist industry started using it to promote New Mexico's natural beauty. It was coined by author Lilian Whiting, who wrote *The Land of Enchantment*, a book about the region published in 1906.

Land of Enchantment State

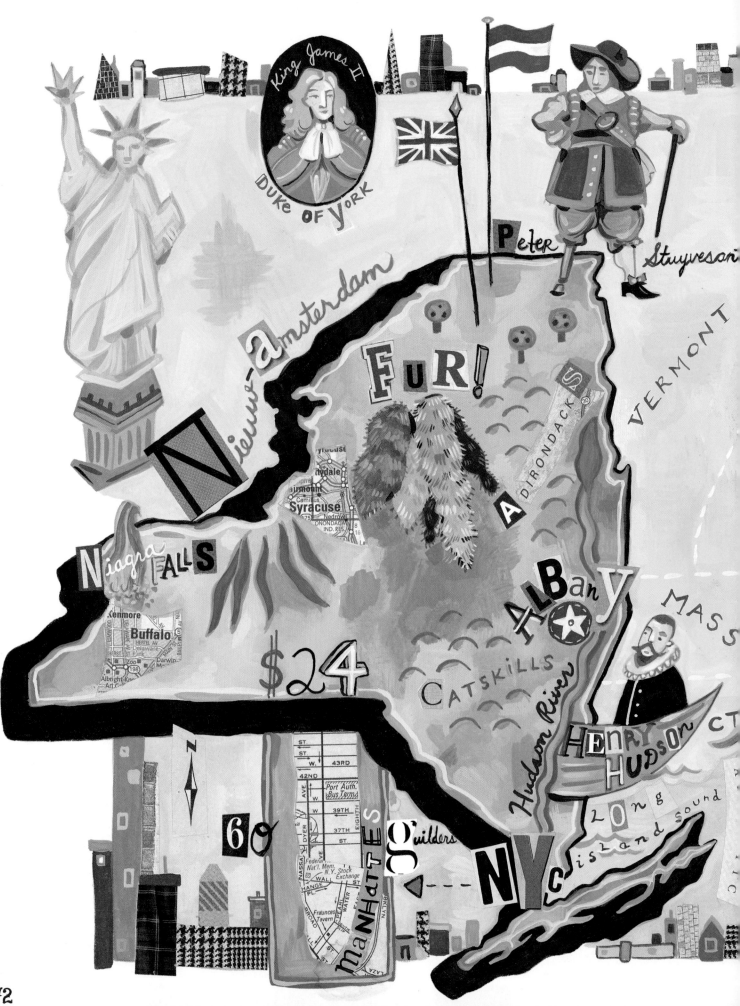

New York

New York: It's all about money and real estate.

In 1609, the English navigator Henry Hudson, working for the Dutch, sailed up the New York river that now bears his name. The good news about New York spread: big place, nice scenery, fertile valleys, good waterways, and fur, fur, fur!

The Dutch established a fur-trading colony and called it Nieuw-Nederland. (Of course, only the Europeans were *nieuw*; native peoples had been in New York for ages.) The colony was governed from Nieuw-Amsterdam, a settlement at the mouth of the Hudson. In 1626, Nieuw-Amsterdam's governing official, Peter Minuit, made the real estate deal of the century — make that centuries! He bought Manhattan, an island owned by native people of the same name, for 60 guilders ($24). Upriver, the Dutch cleared big farms and opened a thriving trading post at Fort Orange, now Albany.

The Dutch ruled for almost 50 years. Then the English decided that everything between the Connecticut and Delaware Rivers belonged to them. Four heavily armed British ships sailed into Nieuw-Amsterdam harbor in August 1664. The English offered a deal: Give up, we'll rule, you go about your business. Peter Stuyvesant, the peg-legged Dutch governor, was hopping mad; everybody else pretty much shrugged. The English took over without a shot and renamed the colony New York, in honor of their Duke of York, who later was crowned King James II.

From 1785 to 1790, New York City was the temporary capital of the new United States. George Washington is said to have called it "the seat of the Empire." The Empire State worked for New Yorkers.

Empire State

North Carolina

Three Kings, two states, one name: Carolina.

Carolina is from *Carolus*, a Latin form for the name *Charles*. In 1562, French explorer Jean Ribaut reached the coast of the Carolinas and named the whole place in honor of Charles IX, the boy-King of France.

The French didn't get a colony going, but in the 1580s, the British tried to. By 1587, they had established a small settlement on Roanoke Island. But by 1590, this "lost colony" had vanished, leaving only a mysterious clue: the word CROATAN carved on a tree.

Just because it was the Kind of place where people disappear didn't mean the British were willing to give up their territorial claim. In 1629 and again in 1663, English Kings bestowed royal charters on some of their faithful noblemen, granting them rights to Carolina. Luckily, both these Kings were called Charles (I and II), so no change of name was required.

Carolina was divided in 1710; by 1729, it was officially two British colonies: North Carolina and South Carolina.

In the 19th century, North Carolina, the Tarheel State, was a big producer of sticky tar and smelly turpentine. According to legend, during a fierce Civil War battle, while other troops fled, a North Carolina regiment bravely stood its ground and won. They later joked that their fellow soldiers needed to put some North Carolina tar on their heels, so they'd stay put in the next fight.

Tarheel State

75

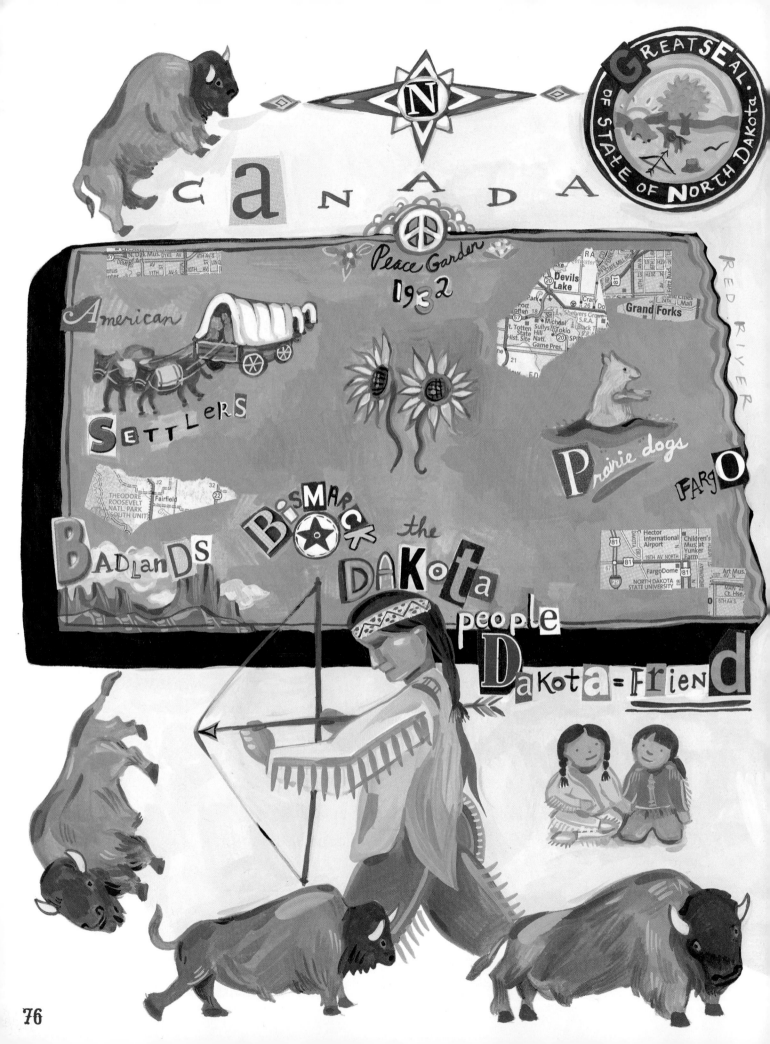

GREAT SEAL · OF THE STATE · OF NORTH DAKOTA

N

CANADA

RED RIVER

Peace Garden 1932

American

Settlers

Badlands

Bismarck

the Dakota people

Dakota = Friend

Prairie dogs

Fargo

North Dakota

North Dakota became our 39th state on November 2, 1889.

For hundreds of years, the great Northern Plains in this midwestern state were home to millions of buffalo and the Native American peoples who hunted them. The Dakota were one of these tribal groups. *Dakota* means "friend" or "ally." When American settlers and soldiers started moving into the area in the 19th century, they called their new-claimed territory Dakota because of the original inhabitants. They also slaughtered the buffalo and changed the Dakota tribal way of life forever.

Congress formally recognized the territory in 1861 and admitted both North Dakota and South Dakota as states in 1889.

North Dakota is one of the few states that every once in a while — say 1947, 1989, 2001 — considers changing its name. Some enterprising Dakotans think North says "too chilly," and that maybe more people would be tempted to move to the state if it was just called Dakota. So far, the measure hasn't passed.

In 1957, the state legislature officially made North Dakota the Peace Garden State. The International Peace Garden straddles the border between North Dakota and Manitoba, Canada. The beautiful garden— with its trees, groves, lakes, and 150,000 flowers—celebrates the friendly relationship between the United States and Canada. The garden was the botanical brainstorm of a Canadian plant scientist, Dr. Henry J. Moore. It opened in 1932.

Peace Garden State

LAKE ERIE

1ST hot dog

BUCKEYE CABIN

ColumBus

Cincinnati

OHIO RiveR

"La Belle Rivière" LARGE beautiful GREAT!

FREEDOM

René Robert CAVELIER

Johnny Appleseed

78

Ohio

The Ohio River flows through American history. In 1669, it brought in René-Robert Cavelier, Sieur de La Salle, the first European to see what he called *la belle rivière*, the beautiful river. Later, the Ohio served as a watery (but temporary) dividing line between encroaching settlers and Native American homelands.

The Ohio River flows through or along the borders of six states: Pennsylvania, West Virginia, Ohio, Kentucky, Indiana, and Illinois, connecting to other important tributaries along the way. In the early 19th century, it was a choice route for pioneers headed west. It was a lot easier to float yourself, your loved ones, and all your stuff on the river than it was to haul it over the Appalachian Mountains. As the territories around the river were settled, the Ohio became an important commercial route for crops and other goods. The river was also the border between slave states and free states. Making it across the Ohio could mean freedom for an escaped slave.

A river this important to this many different people is bound to have more than one name. In fact there are 59 various names or spellings for the 981-mile river. *Ohio* is thought to come from an Iroquois word for "large," "beautiful," or "great river."

Great name for a state, too.

The Buckeye State is named after a tree whose nut looks like a deer's eye. In the 1840 presidential campaign, a newspaper called candidate William Henry Harrison of Ohio a country bumpkin. The down-home idea worked for his campaign; pictures of buckeye-wood canes and cabins became Harrison's symbols. He won.

Buckeye State

OoKLAHoMa!

TRail of TEaRS

the PANhANDLE • RED • PEOPLE •
HUMA ✦ OKLA

OKLaHoMa CiTY

OiL

Twisters

PoW

GREAT SEAL OF THE STATE OF OKLAHOMA • 1907 •

Lawton

Oklahoma

"O-O-O-O-O-Oklahoma, where the wind comes sweepin' down the plain!" is the opening line from the title song of Rodgers and Hammerstein's famous 1943 musical, *Oklahoma!* Lots of people came sweepin' down the plain in this state.

Oklahoma was part of the Indian Territory Congress established in 1830 as a homeland for tribal peoples being pushed off their ancestral lands elsewhere. Cherokee, Chickasaw, Choctaw, Creek, and Seminole peoples were forced to move there; thousands died along this "Trail of Tears." Sixty-seven tribes lived in the territory.

After the Civil War, illegal settlers urged the federal government to officially open up these lands to non-Indian settlers. Instead of traditional tribal rule, a territorial government for the Native American area was proposed. During one meeting about this, Reverend Allen Wright, a New York-educated Choctaw Presbyterian minister, suggested the redefined territory be called Oklahoma. *Okla* in Choctaw means "people"; *huma* (or *humma*) means "red."

The land didn't stay unassigned.

On April 22, 1889, 50,000 cowboys, farmers, laborers, entrepreneurs, and other hopefuls lined up for the first of several Oklahoma land rushes. They came in wagons and buggies. They rode horses, ponies, and mules. When the starting shot cracked, they raced off in a whirlwind of noise and dust to stake their claims in what became our 46th state.

Sooner State

The Sooner State gets its nickname from eager pioneers who jumped the gun, snuck into Oklahoma, and staked land claims "sooner" than land rush rules allowed.

oil

COLUMBIA RIVER

SALEM

Ouragon Ourigan

CASCADES

Ooligan

VITAMIN A

Vitamin C

smelt fish

TRAVELS THROUGH THE INTERIOR PARTS of NORTH AMERICA

1766
1767
1768

82

Oregon

Oregon became our 33rd state on February 14, 1859.

This is the oil,

that came from the fish,

that swam in the river,

that flowed through the northwest,

that gave Oregon its name . . . maybe.

No one knows for sure where the word *Oregon* came from. In 1765, Major Robert Rogers, an enterprising English army officer, wrote of an expedition he proposed to "the River called by the Indians Ouragon." King George II refused to pay for the trip; Major Rogers tried again seven years later with a different spelling, Ourigan. Historians still differ on how and where the officer heard these tribal words and what they mean.

In 1778, Captain Jonathan Carver, an associate of Major Rogers, published a bestseller called *Travels Through the Interior Parts of North America 1766, 1767, and 1768*. He followed Roberts's lead, but reworked the spelling to the River Oregon. Mapmakers went with Oregon when they were labeling what's now the Columbia River.

Recently, two anthropologists have offered a hotly debated new idea. They suggest that the name *Oregon* is linked to *ooligan*, a fish grease Native Americans got from an oily little smelt swimming around in the Northwest. Ooligan was a valuable all-purpose golden oil: you could eat it (Vitamin A! Vitamin C!), light a lamp with it, slather it on as medicine, and barter it.

Castor canadensis, the thick-pelted, tail-slapping, tree-gnawing American beaver, drew fur trappers and traders to Oregon and gave the state its nickname.

Beaver State

83

William PENN

Penn's WOODS Sylvania

NJ

King CHARLES II

HARRISBURG • HERSHEY

Lancaster

Philadelphia

We the People...

MARYLAND

STATE FOREST

FRANKLIN

DE

Pennsylvania

It pays to have a king owe you money.

England's King Charles II had borrowed money from a trusted admiral, Sir William Penn. Penn senior's death meant the King owed his son, William Penn, £16,000.

William Penn, a Quaker, wanted to create what he called a Holy Experiment in the New World, a colony where people could worship freely and participate in their government. King Charles II wanted to expand his empire — and retire his debt at the same time. The royal charter of 1681 solved everything. It gave Penn a large tract of land, which the king decreed should be called Pensilvania, in honor of Admiral Penn. *Sylvania* comes from the Latin word for woods; *Pennsylvania*, as it came to be spelled, means "Penn's woods."

Dutch and Swedish settlers had already moved onto some of the lands that now belonged to William Penn, not to mention all the Native Americans who lived there, too. Penn arrived to establish his new, enlightened colony in 1682. He struck a bold and at the time unusual bargain: Although he held a royal charter for Pennsylvania, Penn and his followers didn't settle it until they had met with tribal leaders and paid the Indians for their land claims. Dealing with his fellow European colonizers was tougher. Penn had to defend his colony against border disputes with Maryland, Delaware, and New Jersey.

A keystone is the essential middle wedge in an arch that holds the whole curve together. The true meaning of Pennsylvania's nickname, the Keystone State, is unknown, but it probably refers to the key position Pennsylvania held as a political, commercial, and geographic center of the 13 American colonies.

Key- stone State

smallest **StAte**

ROODT**E**Y**L**AND**T**

RED ✦ **I**SLAND

Greece

RHODES

PR**oVid**ENCE

West Warwick

116
115
117
Quidnick
Anthony
Washington
33
Nathanael
Greene
Homestead
Tefgue
Lake

SILVERWARE

NARRAGANSETT BAY

STATE of RHODE **I**SLAND & the PROVIDENCE PLANTATIONS

HOPE

1636

cLAmS

N

Newport

Block Island Sound

B**L**OC**K** **I**SLAND

Verrazano

ATLANTIC **O**CEAN

Rhode Island

In 1524, the Italian navigator Giovanni Verrazano sailed north from New York. He spied "an Ilande in the forme of a triangle . . . about the bigness of the Ilande of the Rhodes." Rhodes is an island in Greece.

In 1614, Adriaen Block, an intrepid Dutch explorer and fur trader, also explored the region. He named Block Island, the largest of 35 islands in Rhode Island's waters, after himself. When he sailed into the Narragansett Bay, he noted the "fiery aspect" of its red clay shoreline and wrote *Roodt Eylandt* (red island) on his charts.

Here's where tracking this state's name gets tricky.

Verrazano was actually talking about Block Island; Block may have been talking about Rhode Island. Then in 1636, Roger Williams fled Puritan-controlled Massachusetts. The clergyman bought some land from the Narragansett and called his new home Providence as thanks to his god. *Plantations* was added because that's an old English word for colony. Williams thought Verrazano's Rhodes reference was to Aquidneck Island, another part of the growing new colony. Aquidneck became Rhode Island in 1644.

By 1663, what is now our smallest state had its really big name: The State of Rhode Island and Providence Plantations. That's what it was called in the royal charter granted by England's King Charles II. It guaranteed Roger Williams's dream: There would be "full libertie in religious concernements" in Rhode Island.

Rhode Island, the Ocean State, has only 1,045 square miles of land, but 384 miles of shoreline along the Atlantic Ocean and Narragansett Bay. That puts all its residents about 30 miles, or a half-hour away, from the water — not counting summer beach traffic!

Ocean State

South Carolina

Native Americans, Spanish explorers, French soldiers and sailors, British noblemen, immigrants from Barbados and Viriginia, even *pirates*, all wanted a piece of the action in what became two adjoining southern states: North Carolina and South Carolina.

The Carolinas were once one big territory called Carolina in honor of a French and then two British kings, all named Charles. Thousands of Native Americans already called the place home before the Europeans arrived in the 16th century. The Spanish sailed in first, followed by the French. Each got to first base in the colonial game: claim and name. It was the English who scored. A British royal charter of 1663 spelled out their claim to all land, coast, and waterways in the geographic area between 36 and 31 degrees northern latitude — not to mention the "whales, sturgeons, and all other royal fishes in the sea" there.

Like the French, the British called the region Carolina after their monarch. But unlike their European competitors, the English moved in and stayed. One British settlement became a thriving port and the colony's capital. It too got the royal treatment when it came to names: Charles Town (now Charleston).

How to become a state nickname:
1. Grow some palmetto trees.
2. Cut down these trees.
3. Use the palmetto wood to build a fort on Sullivan's Island to protect Charleston.
4. Get attacked by British warships on June 28, 1776, during the Revolutionary War.
5. Win the battle because the fort's palmetto tree walls aborbed the shock of cannonballs and held.
6. Become the Palmetto State.

Palmetto State

South Dakota

Dakota is a tribal word for "friend" or "ally." But when it came to statehood, the north and south parts of the Dakota Territory were more like feuding twins.

In 1883, the settlers in southern Dakota were outraged when the territory's capital shifted from Yankton to Bismarck, which was in the northern part of the territory. The north was more populated. Folks up there thought the capital should go where the people are. There had already been talk of breaking up the Dakota Territory into two; now the rumbling, grumbling, and politicking to recognize South Dakota got really loud.

A congressional bill in 1889 created the states of North Dakota and South Dakota. Once President Benjamin Harrison signed the documents, the 39th and 40th states would join the Union. There was just one big, politically loaded question: North or south, who would be admitted first?

President Harrison wisely asked his Secretary of State to shuffle the papers so he couldn't see which he was signing. Both North Dakota and South Dakota became states on November 2, 1889.

Nobody knows which twin was born first. (The Dakotas are numbered based on alphabetical order.)

You can't miss the namesake for this state's nickname, the Mount Rushmore State. Five hundred feet up a mountain face in the Black Hills are sculptures of George Washington, Thomas Jefferson, Theodore Roosevelt, and Abraham Lincoln. Each presidential head carved on Mount Rushmore is 60 feet high.

Mount Rushmore State

91

Tennessee

"The U.S. Territory South of the River Ohio" is a little long to stamp on license plates or print on key chains, coffee mugs, and baseball caps. Of course, there were no cars or souvenir stands in 1790, when this name was in use. But lucky for today's tchotchke manufacturers, by the time this territory became our 16th state, its citizens were using a shorter name: Tennessee.

Everyone agrees that Tennessee comes from a Native American word, but no one is quite sure how, when, or where. Captain Juan Pardo, a Spanish explorer, reached an Indian village called Tanasqui in 1567. A couple of centuries later, settlers ventured near two neighboring Cherokee river villages, Tanasqui or Tanase. People started calling the waterway the Tennessee River. Next thing you know, in the 1750s, James Glen, the governor of nearby South Carolina, is penning letters referring to the region as Tennessee.

It's easy to hear how Native American words like *Tansqui* or *Tanasi* glide into Tennessee. But what these tribal words meant to their original speakers is lost in history.

When duty called, Tennesseans answered. That's why it's nicknamed the Volunteer State. During the War of 1812, volunteer soldiers from this state marched on down to help General Andrew Jackson trounce the British in the Battle of New Orleans.

Volunteer State

93

Texas

Howdy! Welcome to the state whose motto is friendship and whose name means nearly the same thing.

Texas comes from *taysha*, a Caddo word for "friend," or "ally." The Caddo were a confederacy of native peoples who lived and farmed the river valleys of parts of Texas, Louisiana, Arkansas, and Oklahoma. When Spanish explorers first trekked through these Caddo lands and into Texas in the 16th century, they were impressed with the confederacy's organization and civilization — and with the fact that these tribes were less hostile than other native peoples they encountered. The Spanish called the Caddo the "great kingdom of Tejas," their interpretation of the "friend" word, and named their first mission in the area San Francisco de los Tejas in 1690. Eventually, the name *Tejas* evolved into *Texas*.

After that, Texas was pretty much called Texas, right on into statehood.

The Lone Star State gets its nickname from the Texan flag. The single, or lone, star on this flag is said to represent Texans' stand-alone struggle for independence. Single stars appeared on various flags of the Republic of Texas and waved at many a battle, including the decisive Battle of San Jacinto in 1836. The Texan army led by General Sam Houston defeated General Antonio López de Santa Anna's Mexican army. Texas then became independent of Mexican rule.

Lone Star State

INDUSTRY

THE GREAT SEAL OF THE STATE OF UTAH

INDUSTRY
1847
1896

GREAT SALT LAKE

SALT LAKE CITY

Uinta Mountains

MORMONS

CHURCH of the LATTER DAY SAINTS

BOOK of MORMON

Hunters & gatherers

the UTE Bands

Utah

The Ute, a group of 12 loosely connected Native American bands, were hunters and gatherers whose traditional lands stretched across what is now Colorado and Utah. *Ute* is interpreted to mean "land of the sun" or "high-up." It's a reference to the often mountainous areas the Ute inhabited or hunted in. From Ute came Utah — literally, once settlers started displacing these native peoples.

In 1847, members of the Church of Jesus Christ of Latter-Day Saints, seeking religious freedom, began moving to Utah in large groups. These pioneers were commonly called Mormons; they settled in Ute lands.

The Mormons quickly cleared and planted farmlands and built thriving communities. In a few short years, they were ready and eager for statehood. In fact, they organized their own Territory of Deseret. *Deseret* comes from the religious text, the *Book of Mormon*; it means honeybee. The Mormon pioneers were a close-knit society that valued cooperation, hard work, and shared goals and values. They often used a beehive as a metaphor for themselves or their beliefs.

The Mormons petitioned Congress to be admitted as the Territory of Deseret in 1849. Congress approved the territorial request in 1850, but as the Territory of Utah.

There are two giant bronze beehives with buzzing bees at the steps of Utah's State Capitol Building. That's because Utah is the Beehive State. You'll see dome-shaped beehives, the symbol of industriousness, all over Utah on buildings, road signs, ads, the state flag, police cars, even on the doorknobs in the Capitol building.

Beehive State

Samuel Champlain

LAKE CHAMPLAIN

GREEN MOUNTAINS

GREEN MTS.

MONTPELIER

New Connecticut...

State of Vermont

1777

Ethan Allen

& the GREEN MOUNTAIN BOYS

Vermont

In July 1609, French explorer and geographer Samuel Champlain and his party of nine Frenchmen and 60 Huron and Algonquian sailed into a big beautiful lake. He named it after himself, Lake Champlain, and claimed all he saw for France, including the mountain range in the distance, *les Verts Monts* . . . the Green Mountains.

Call it like you see it, Sam.

More than 150 years later, the colonies of New Hampshire and New York both laid claim to the region Champlain visited, which was by now called the New Hampshire Grants. Feisty local citizen Ethan Allen formed his famous Green Mountain Boys to fight off the "Yorkers" they feared would overrun the region's original settlers.

In 1777, delegates from the New Hampshire Grants met and declared the region a republic called New Connecticut. Dr. Thomas Young, a Philadelphia scholar and statesman, and friend of Ethan Allen's, urged New Connecticut to join the other 13 American colonies that had declared independence. Young suggested New Connecticut write a state constitution and change its name to Vermont, in honor of the mountains and the boys. The idea got the *vert* light; the republic became Vermont on June 30, 1777.

Vermont, the Green Mountain State, is nicknamed after:

○ The mountain range that's made of green-colored shale and runs most of the length of the state.

○ The state and Revolutionary War heroes Ethan Allen and the Green Mountain Boys.

○ Both

Green Mountain State

99

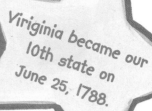

Virginia

Once upon a time there was a brilliant 16th-century British queen named Elizabeth I. Since she was unmarried, everyone called her the Virgin Queen. One of Elizabeth's favorite members of her court was the pirate-fighting, poetry-writing, dashing soldier and explorer Sir Walter Raleigh.

Raleigh dreamed of gold, silver, and a thriving English colony in the "New World." His queen liked the idea of expanding her empire to the American continent. More fame! More riches! A chance to beat out her royal rivals in Spain and Portugal!

On March 25, 1584, Elizabeth signed a charter giving Raleigh the right "to discover . . . and view such remote . . . and barbarous lands . . . not actually possessed of any Christian Prince." In other words, he should lay claim to anything the Spanish and Portuguese hadn't already snatched up. (Of course, there already were thousands of native peoples living in these supposedly "barbarous lands.")

Between 1585 and 1587, Raleigh, along with several other noblemen and merchants, sponsored three expeditions to America. The ships reached what is now the coast of North Carolina. Raleigh claimed and named the whole region Virginia, in honor of his queen.

Raleigh's Roanoke colonies failed, but the name *Virginia* stayed on the map.

Dominion means complete ownership of a place. Virginia is the Old Dominion because England's King Charles II thought so highly of his colony that sometime around 1663, he added it to his shield, making Virginia the equal of France, Ireland, and Scotland. It's also known as the Mother of Presidents, since 7 of the first 12 U.S. presidents came from there.

Old Dominion State

The SEAL of the STATE of WASHINGTON

1889

PUGET SOUND

trout

SEAttle

CASCADES

ROCKIES

red

apples

Columbia River

PIONEERS

MT. SAINT HELENS

OLYMPIA

MT. RAINIER
Sunrise Visitor Ctr.
Mt. Rainier
Pt. in Wash.
14,411
NATL.
PARK
Paradise
CLOSED

COLUMBIA TERRITORY

OREGON

Univer
Pla

Steilacoom
Tribal
Cultural Ctr.

Steilacoom

La

FT. LEWIS
MILITARY RES.

Seattle
Bremerton
Port Orchard

Burien

KITSAP

Kirkland

102

Washington

In the 1850s, this state was part of the vast Oregon Territory (think Oregon, Washington, Idaho, and part of Montana, *put together!*). The territory was just a little too big and unwieldy for its northernmost citizens.

On August 29, 1851, 27 disgruntled pioneers who lived north of the Columbia River met at Cowlitz Landing. They wrote a petition to Congress, complaining that it was cheaper to travel all the way from St. Louis, Missouri, to Boston, Massachusetts, than it was for North Oregonians to head on down south and see a clerk or judge in the government seat of their own territory. The pioneers wanted to carve out a new region with a separate government; they called it Columbia Territory.

Congress considered the petition. They were okay with the idea of splitting the Oregon Territory, but the name? It could be confusing, since there already was a District of Columbia. Washington Territory was substituted, so there would be "a sovereign State bearing the name of the Father of his Country." The bill passed on February 10, 1853, making Washington the only state named after a U.S. president . . . and the only one that has to keep adding "state" after its name.

There already was a Washington, too.

Charles Tallmadge Conover was a real-estate entrepreneur in Seattle, Washington, at the turn of the 20th century. He also chaired the publicity committee of the Chamber of Commerce. Conover nicknamed Washington the Evergreen State after its richly forested lands.

Evergreen State

West Virginia

The Civil War that divided the nation also divided Virginia.

Up until 1861 Virginia and West Virginia were one big but not-so-happy state. East Virginians tended to be slaveholding owners of large plantations. West Virginians owned smaller properties, if they owned land at all; slavery was not as widespread. State government, tax and voting rules, and services usually favored East Virginia.

In 1861, the Civil War broke out, and Virginia voted to secede from the Union. The western part of the state voted to secede from Virginia. Delegates met at a constitutional convention on December 3, 1861, and agreed their new state should remain part of the Union. They didn't agree on what to call it. The top contenders:

Kanawha

Pros

- It's an Indian word for "place of white stone," which refers to local salt deposits.
- States name themselves after rivers and there are two Kanawha Rivers here.
- It's got a soft and musical sound.

Cons

- The post office will get confused: There already is a Kanawha County.
- Voters hate it.

Allegheny

Pros

- Nice, scenic mountain range in the state.

Cons

- What about the places that aren't near the mountains?

The vote? Allegheny, 2; Kanawha, 9; West Virginia, 30.

West Virginia

Pros

- Love the name, love its history, and westerners have a right to it, too.
- Already a familiar name.

Cons

- Doesn't sound like a clean break.

Pretty much all of West Virginia is mountainous, hence its nickname, the Mountain State.

Mountain State

Wisconsin

Wisconsin became our 30th state on May 29, 1848.

Our 30th state is named after a river that not even two Frenchmen on the same expedition spelled the same way.

The Wisconsin River flows for 430 miles; it's the largest river in the state. In 1673, the fur-trapper Louis Jolliet and the missionary Father Jacques Marquette paddled along exploring what Marquette called the Meskousing in his journal; he also wrote *Miskous* in another reference. Meanwhile, his partner Jolliet inked in *Miskonsing* on a map he drew a year later.

Fast-forward nine years and another French explorer, René-Robert Cavelier, Sieur de La Salle, claims the local native peoples call the river Ouisconsing, or Misconsing. Ouisconsing was in pretty common use until the 19th century, when the Americans moved in, especially when there was a lead mining rush in 1825. They slowly "Americanized" the name and officially organized the region as the Wisconsin Territory in 1836. But free-form spelling didn't die. Various newspaper editors and even the territorial governor liked Wiskonsan better, so they used it.

Depending on how you pronounce it or spell it, Wisconsin may come from tribal words meaning "red stone river" or "great stone river."

The Badger State is named after an animal, but a two-footed one. In the 1800s, lead miners tunneled through southwest Wisconsin. They even dug out caves to sleep in. People called the miners "badgers," after the fierce, furry, burrowing mammal with 2-inch claws that could dig a hole and disappear in minutes.

Wyoming

Why Wyoming? Because Arapaho, Big Horn, Cheyenne, Lincoln, Platte, Shoshoni, Sweetwater, Sioux, and Yellowstone were rejected by the U.S. Senate when it organized the Wyoming Territory in 1868.

That was all right with most of the mountain men, miners, ranchers, farmers, and other settlers in what became our 44th state — they already called the place Wyoming.

Long before Americans headed west looking for beaver pelts, gold, and wide-open spaces to raise crops or cattle, Wyoming had been home to at least 13 Native American tribes. These nomadic Plains Indians followed the huge buffalo herds that grazed in the region's grassy prairies. Buffalo provided tribal people with everything from food to fuel. Wyoming comes from *mecheweamiing* or *mecheweami-ing*, Algonquian for "at the big flats" or "on the great plain."

Once the wagon trains started rolling through and the U.S. military and its buffalo hunters followed, *mecheweamiing* gave way to Wyoming — and the Plains Indians' way of life was eventually destroyed.

Wyoming, the Cowboy State, trademarked the picture of a cowboy on a bucking horse that it uses on things like the state license plate. Buckaroos have flocked there to the world's largest outdoor rodeo since 1897.

Wyoming is also called the Equality State because in 1869 the territorial legislature passed the country's first female suffrage bill, specifically and permanently giving women the right to vote.

Cowboy State

Washington, D.C.

Washington, D.C., the capital of the United States, is both the city of Washington and the District of Columbia.

In the early days of the nation, Congress met in eight different cities: Philadelphia, Baltimore, Lancaster, York, Princeton, Annapolis, Trenton, and New York. But some legislators had a capital idea: Let's establish a real, permanent capital.

Maryland and Virginia ceded lands along the Potomac River to Congress; the 10 square miles were first called Federal City. On July 16, 1790, Congress declared the city of Washington in the District of Columbia the permanent capital of the United States. The city was officially named Washington on September 9, 1791, in honor of George Washington, the hero of the Revolutionary War and the unanimously elected first president of the nation. The District of Columbia's name comes from a Latin word form related to the explorer Christopher Columbus.

Its nickname? What else? D.C.

111

Web Sites

Official State Sites

All 50 states have their own Web sites; so does Washington, D.C. These sites usually have general information about the history and geography of the state, its symbols, flag, motto, and official designations. They also have links to other important sites, such as the state library or historical society and official tourism sites.

Alabama
www.alabama.gov/

Alaska
www.state.ak.us/

Arizona
www.az.gov/

Arkansas
www.state.ar.us/

California
www.ca.gov/

Colorado
www.colorado.gov/

Connecticut
www.ct.gov/

Delaware
www.delaware.gov/

Florida
www.myflorida.com/

Georgia
www.georgia.gov/

Hawaii
www.hawaii.gov/

Idaho
www.state.id.us/

Illinois
www.illinois.gov/

Indiana
www.in.gov/

Iowa
www.iowa.gov/

Kansas
www.accesskansas.org/

Kentucky
www.kentucky.gov/

Louisiana
www.louisiana.gov/

Maine
www.state.me.us/

Maryland
www.maryland.gov/

Massachusetts
www.mass.gov/

Michigan
www.michigan.gov/

Minnesota
www.state.mn.us/

Mississippi
www.mississippi.gov/

Missouri
www.mo.gov/

Montana
http://mt.gov/

Nebraska
www.nebraska.gov/

Nevada
www.nv.gov/

New Hampshire
www.nh.gov/

New Jersey
www.state.nj.us/

New Mexico
www.newmexico.gov/

New York
www.ny.gov/

North Carolina
www.ncgov.com/

North Dakota
www.nd.gov/

Ohio
http://ohio.gov/

Oklahoma
www.ok.gov/

Oregon
www.oregon.gov/

Pennsylvania
www.state.pa.us/

Rhode Island
www.state.ri.us/

South Carolina
www.sc.gov/

South Dakota
www.state.sd.us/

Tennessee
www.state.tn.us/

Texas
www.state.tx.us/

Utah
www.utah.gov/

Vermont
www.vermont.gov/

Virginia
www.virginia.gov/

Washington
http://access.wa.gov/

West Virginia
www.wv.gov/

Wisconsin
www.wisconsin.gov/

Wyoming
http://wyoming.gov/

Washington, D.C.
www.dc.gov/